2 Graves

by Paul Sellar

First presented at The Pleasance Theatre, Edinburgh on 6 August 2006
Transferred to London's West End on 1 November 2006, where it opened
the newly refurbished Arts Theatre

Andy Jordan Productions

Founded in 2000, having evolved from Andy Jordan's previous new writing company, Bristol Express. Recent shows include *Picasso's Women* (with Jerry Hall, Susannah York, Josie Lawrence, Gwen Taylor, Cherie Lunghi: National Theatre, Edinburgh Festival, Far East, UK tour in co-production with ATG, 2000 / 2001 / 2002), *Oxygen* (with Catherine Cusack, Robert Demeger: Riverside Studios), *Murder in Paris* (with Louise Jameson, Michael Siberry, Ian Cullen: co-production with Basingstoke Haymarket Theatre), *My Matisse* (with Daisy Bates, Helen Grace, Tina Gray), *Kings of the Road* (with James Ellis, Ed Byrne: Edinburgh Festival, Greenwich Theatre, Dublin Ambassador), *Last Song of the Nightingale* (with Tracie Bennett: Edinburgh Festival, Greenwich Theatre), *Three on a Couch* (with Leigh Zimmerman, Michael Praed), *Calculus* (with Nick Wilton, John Kane, David Gant: New End Theatre), *Talk About The Passion* (with Phillipa Peak, Dan Ainsleigh), *Phallacy* (with Karen Archer, Jack Klaff), *Hush* (with Juliet Cowan, Alex Palmer: Edinburgh Festival, Arcola Theatre), *Playing Burton* (with Brian Mallon), *Rosebud: The Lives of Orson Welles* (with Christian McKay, co-produced with Steven Berkoff: Kings Head Theatre), *Taboos* (with Nicola Bryant) and *Lies Have Been Told* (with Philip York, New End Theatre, West End Trafalgar Studios, 2 Seasons, 2005 / 2006).

Andy Jordan Productions Ltd
ANDYJAndyjordan@aol.com

Andy Jordan Productions

2 Graves

by Paul Sellar

Performed by Jonathan Moore

Director **Yvonne McDevitt**
Designers **Kimie Nakano & Matthew Deely**
Lighting Designer **Colin Grenfell**
Sound Designer **Kay Basson**
Assistant Director **Nick Blackburn**
Stage Manager **Carla Archer**
Chair made by **Penny Spedding**

Producer **Andy Jordan**
General Manager **Christopher Corner**
Press Representation **Kevin Wison PR** 020 7430 2060
Marketing **Mobius Industries**
Graphic Design **The GP Design Partnership** 020 7379 4300

Thanks to Vanessa Dunley, Rosa Wyatt, Anne Aldred, Andy Beardmore, Lucien and Will at Factory Settings, Nick Green, Paul Stephens, The People Show, and all those whose help came too late to be mentioned here.

The author would like to thank the director Kenneth Bentley and the performer Andrew Dickens for their excellent work on *The Damage*; two back-to-back monologues about gambling and sport which became the basis for the first half of *2 Graves*.

Company Biographies

Paul Sellar *Writer*

Paul studied drama at Bristol University. Theatre includes: *The Bedsit* (featuring James Ellis; at the Tabard Theatre before transferring to the BAC as part of the Time Out Critics' Choice Season; later that year the play was produced by and at the Assembly Rooms for the Edinburgh festival); *World's End* (rehearsed reading National theatre Studio, then a workshop reading at The Bush followed by staged reading at the Old Vic; the play is currently in development and is scheduled for production in 2007); *The Damage* (Soho TC Previews /Edinburgh festival); *Dark Is The Night* (stage adaptations of *The Night Wire* and *The Waxwork* which formed a double bill of mystery and suspense). *Cell G159*, later revived as *The Dead Move Fast* (featuring Sylvester McCoy; Gilded Balloon, Edinburgh Festival / The Arts Theatre, West End as a 'Showcase presentation'). His commissions include National theatre, Gilded Balloon productions, Camden Young People's theatre and Central School of Speech and Drama. His work has also been produced in Dublin and Chicago. *The Bedsit* is published by Faber and Faber and *The Dead Move Fast* is published by Oberon Books.

Jonathan Moore *Jack*

Jonathan Moore is a popular theatre and television actor and an award-winning opera director/librettist, playwright, and theatre director. He co-starred with Gabriel Byrne in his own play *Treatment* (BBC Films, which won one of his two Fringe First Awards). He has played leading roles on TV/film including *Jack The Ripper* (CBS) *Bleak House*, in two series of *Roger Roger*, the series *Inside Story*, *The People's Harry Enfield, Foyle's*

War, Dalziel & Pascoe, Lovejoy and many others. Leading roles in theatre include: *Round The Horne* (West End and tour), Banquo in *Macbeth* (Arcola), Shakespeare in *School of Night* (Chichester), Julius in Shaw's *Misalliance* (Chichester), Bottom in *Midsummer Night's Dream* (Arcola), Henry Fielding in *The Art of Success* (RSC), Titok in *The Gorky Brigade* (Royal Court), Skylight in *Class Enemy* (Young Vic), Nick in *Dead Funny* (Salisbury Playhouse and Theatr Clwyd), Smerdyakov in *Brothers Karamazov* (Royal Exchange). His own stage plays include *Treatment* (Gate & Donmar), *Street Captives* (Edinburgh Fringe/Manchester Royal Exchange/Gate Theatre), *Behind Heaven* (Royal Exchange/London Donmar), *Regeneration* (Half Moon) and *This Other Eden* (Soho Theatre). In opera he is one of our most innovative directors, known for his world premieres of works by composers Mark-Anthony Turnage, Michael Nyman, James Macmillan, Stewart Copeland, Ian McQueen, Henze, Schnittke, Ludovico Einaudi and Muller-Wieland (ENO, Scottish Opera, Venice La Fenice, Munich, BonnOpera, Opera North, Barbados, Teatro Principale Valencia, Darmstadt, Basle). He recently directed *Sex, Chips And Rock 'n' Roll* (Royal Exchange). Opera librettos include the film *Horse Opera*, which he also acted in, *East And West*, which he also directed (Almeida) and *Greek* (Munich Biennale Best Libretto Award). Other awards include Royal Philharmonic Society Award for Best Film for *Greek*, Munich Biennale Best Director Award for *63: Dream Palace*, and an Olivier Award nomination for *Greek* at the ENO. He previously performed in a Fringe First winning one man play about Thomas Chatterton, *I Die For None Of Them* by J E Cox. This is Jonathan's first time back at The

Arts since he directed the premiere of *Demonstration of Affection* by Chris Ward.

Yvonne McDevitt *Director*

Yvonne McDevitt is an Irish director based in London. Her critically acclaimed productions of *Not I* and *Rockaby* by Samuel Beckett toured to the Hermitage Theatre in Moscow in 1997. Her 2002 production of *Exiles* by James Joyce at the Young Vic Theatre, the first since Harold Pinter's 1971 production, was awarded a Jerwood Director's Award. Her productions of *On War* inspired by Claude von Clausewitz, at the Young Vic Theatre and *Marching Song* by John Whiting at the National Theatre Studio, were staged in 2003. Her radical devised work, *Brussels Manifesto* was produced in 2005 at the Scarabeus Theatre in the Turkish quarter of Brussels. She has just been awarded an unprecedented grant from the Arts Council of England for her production of *The Bitter Tears Of Petra Von Kant* by Rainer Werner Fassbinder for 2007. The Oslo Experiment, a new devised work inspired by Ingmar Bergman's *Scenes From a Marriage* is currently being developed for production in Oslo in 2008. Her most recent devised work, *I Only Want You To Love Me* was staged at Theatre 503 in London in May. She is about to direct *Not I*, *Footfalls* and *Come And Go* at the Theatre Nationale Populaire in Lyon. Yvonne was awarded the Judith E Wilson Drama Fellowship at the University of Cambridge in 2004.

Matthew Deely *Co-Designer*

Attended Motley Theatre Design Course, was Associate Set Designer with Stefanos Lazaridis on many operas in the UK and Europe. The most notable of these included *Julietta* (Opera North), *Faust* (Munich), *Lohengrin* (Bayreuth Festival), *A Midsummer Night's Dream* (Venice),

Wozzeck and *The Ring Cycle* (Royal Opera House). He designed *Marriage of Figaro* (ENO), *Uganda* (NT Studio), *Romans in Britain* (Man on the Moon). He was Video Artist on *Lady of the Drowned* (Southwark Playhouse). Currently designing Samuel Beckett plays, directed by Yvonne McDevitt at TNP Lyon. Film credits include Assistant Art Director on *Proof* (Miramax), Art Department, *Closer* (Elstree Studios) and *Margate Exodus* (Artangel).

Kimie Nakano *Co-Designer*

Studied theatre costume at ENSATT in Paris and theatre design at Wimbledon School of Art. She was Assistant Designer at Opera de Paris, the Saito Kinen Festival, Japan, and for the film *Eight And A Half Women* by Peter Greenaway. She has designed the Award-winning *Yabu no naka*, directed by Mansai Nomura at the Japan Art Festival 1999 and a collaboration with Megumi Nakamura, *Sand Flower* received the Gold Award at the Maastricht Festival 2000. Many designs in the UK include productions for Polka Theatre, The Britten Festival and Yellow Earth Theatre Company. Currently designing Samuel Beckett plays, directed by Yvonne McDevitt at TNP Lyon. Directorial credits include: *Snow* (Workshop) at ENO studio and *8:15* for Ballet Rambert.

Andy Jordan *Producer*

Works as a director and producer in theatre, TV, film and radio. Created the acclaimed multi-award-winning Bristol Express Theatre Co. for whom he directed/produced over 100 new plays. Is one of the UK's leading directors/ producers of new writing, and is particularly renowned for discovering and helping to develop literally hundreds of new writers, many of whom are now internationally recognised. He has a long association with the Edinburgh Festival, having

won a number of Festival Awards
and produced/directed a huge range
of straight plays, comedy, music and
one person shows, many of which
introduced artists who are now
household names. Freelance theatre
directing credits includes many UK
repertory theatres; London's West End,
Off-West End and Fringe; national and
international touring; and theatre and
radio in New York. He trained in TV &
Film at the BBC, and was a founder
of one of the earliest independent
TV production companies, Playfair
Productions. In radio, where he was
a Senior Radio Drama Producer for
the BBC, he is one of the UK's leading
audio producers, having directed
numerous internationally award-
winning productions (two International
Sony Radio Awards, two Giles Cooper
Awards, the New York Radio Festival
Award and the European Union
Broadcasting Award). He also teaches,
and is currently a Senior Lecturer in
Drama at Lincoln University, and was
formerly Head of Drama at Bradfield
College. He founded Andy Jordan
Productions Ltd in 2000.

Christopher Corner
General Manager

A freelance Administrator and
Production Manager specialising in
new writing, Chris has worked for most
of the major new writing companies
including Foco Novo, Joint Stock, Bristol
Express, Paines Plough, Bright Red,
Moving Theatre, Escape Artists, The
Half Moon and The Wedding Collective.
Also with York Early Music Festival,
Leicester Haymarket, Sheffield Crucible,
the Royal Court and the Royal Opera
House. Manager of The Wrestling
School, a company that tours the
work of Howard Barker in Europe, and
Consultant General Manager for Kali
Theatre. Chris is also a visiting lecturer
at London South Bank University.

Paul Sellar

2 GRAVES

OBERON BOOKS
LONDON

First published in 2006 by Oberon Books Ltd
521 Caledonian Road, London N7 9RH
Tel: 020 7607 3637 / Fax: 020 7607 3629
e-mail: info@oberonbooks.com
www.oberonbooks.com

A catalogue record for this book is available from the British
Library.

Cover photograph by Hugo Glendinning.

Graphic design by the GP Design Partnership.

ISBN: 1 84002 713 4 / 978-1-84002-713-6

Printed in Great Britain by Antony Rowe Ltd, Chippenham.

For my parents

2 Graves

There's a poetry to justice when a wrong is avenged
Yes it's often said – among the dead –
That there is no heaven…
No heaven higher than revenge

It's late – 1988
And we're off to settle a score
A fellah named Ron,
had done us wrong
ten long years before

At the 1978
World Professional Darts
Championship. The title at stake
And Dad was in with a shout
'bout that make no mistake

See 1978 was known as Dad's last dance
It's folklore round our table
My mum gave him one last chance
To crack it if he was able
Or get a job that's stable

So every day at half-past-five
I'd go down to the garage
Plug in the heater
Reset the meter
Seems times were tight, though Dad'd large
It up when underground. And, yes, he'd done
A few jobs in his time.

But that was all behind him now

I felt for my old man
Though I felt for my mum too
But dad was doing all he can
What more's a man supposed to do?

Once you've done time you see
They're wary to take you on
Don't matter how right you might be
They just say the timing's wrong

'Had you called the other day…'
Or – 'Bobby – I've just let three go'
'Things are rough,' 'times are tough'
'And business ain't half slow'

Hard not to take it personal
It amounts to a form of abuse
You'd rather hear the truth, warts 'n all
Than some peddled out excuse.

It was dead round our way
A cul-de-sac of breaking hearts
Stuffed with vice and bustle
And scrap and hustle and Dad's
One way out was darts.

So.

The heater purred and filled the room
I'd get his cans of beer
Dad's voice emerged from out the gloom.
'Cor, it's warm as toast in here.'

He'd flick on the lights
I'd clear up a bit
Bin the empties
Empty out the ashtray
He'd put his fags on the table
I'd get a bag of crisps
He chalked up the board
I'd keep the score.

Then he'd stand there warming up
Just a few looseners
The arrows would fly
Before long he'd be dead on song
Ton forties no trouble

Never missed a double
And if it was under 121 he'd take it on

Keeping score
I'd look on

Keeping an eye on the stance
The grip
The approach
The follow-through
The flight
If he missed, I'd chip in
A sort of self-appointed coach
'Don't look so sound tonight Dad
Not so steady
Not quite pushing through the line
Think you're rushing, take your time
Wait till you're good and ready.'
'Was I rushing?' he'd ask
'You were falling over on that double nine.'

He was only semi-pro
But he had what it took to go all the way

He'd won a few locals
Led for the pub and had built up some renown
Amongst those in the know anyway,
Those who know what's going down

And pretty soon – word got round
There was whispering that followed him to town

'He's a bit good that Bobby Tops…'
'Got a steady hand and all the shots –'
'You reckon he can take it on?'
'Well, he's in with a shout if he can get past Ron.'

Dad was on fire
My face lit up with pride
As he punched in four 180s
On his way past Michael Smythe

Next man up was Charlie Drake
As good a shot as any
He threw damn well and only fell
'cos he took on one shot too many

They came, they went
They came again
But Dad had found his game
And those that thought him written off
Were made to think again

Through the prelim rounds he went
Took 'em at a stroll
Things were opening up for him
Dad was on a roll

And in town
Word got round

'You know that bloke
drinks down the Star and Garter
I saw him win
Three on the spin
And that was just for starters.'

And so on and so forth
The buzz had begun

All those hours dad had spent
The blood, the sweat, the tears
The days, the months, the weeks,
The nights
The nights, the days, the years
The cursings and the failings
The cold, the fags, the beers,
It all looked sure to end
But dad threw great in '78
And he started to make amends

No more the man who could have been
No more the man that weren't
No more the bloke who packed it in

No more the pain that hurt
No more the first round loss
No more life's early bath
No more the angry sullen toss
Of the sad defeated dart.

No more tears from mum at night
No more the rows upstairs
No more the ugly sounds of fights
No more the 'I don't cares'
No more the cowed departure
No more the head hung low
No more the binge thereafter
No more the sad no show

No more the days of shame
No more the weeks of woe
No more the 'Whatshisname?'
No more 'least he had a go'

No. Now

It's 'here comes Bobby'

No. Now

It's 'boys – watch out'
There's a real pro-Bob lobby
What thinks he's got a shout

The odds were something stupid
But now they're slashed to bits
The bookies saw him throw like Cupid
And they got the bleeding shits

Bring him in from 150
Call him to 12 to 1
Hot favourite's still Big Ronnie
But we was – 'Bring it on!'

Now Ronnie was a top flight boy
He could pull a crowd or two

He could mix it with the very best
And still find some way through

A few years back
Along with Filky and Nethers
Big Ron first burst upon the stage
He shot his way to the semis at the first attempt
There was a lot of press coverage
Which was good, 'cos there was a lot of Ron

He'd made the semis twice
He was well known on the box
He weren't afraid of no one
And not of Bobby Tops

So the family pulled together
Mum working on his cape
It was soft black treated leather
Which she tapered into shape

His name was stitched in pink and gold
It ran across his back
It said Bobby Tops in big bold blocks
And was echoed on his cap

We thought he should make an entrance, see?
Stand out on the box
They'd love him on TV
He had long, blonde flowing locks

Bottle bronze complexion
Big blue shining eyes
And a jewellery selection
Of a weight-defying size

But the *pièce de resistance*
The bit we loved the best
Was not the gold around his fingers
But the gold around his neck
Three pounds five ounces
It'd make King Midas blush

The thickest chain you've ever seen
And if you pulled it, it'd flush

He looked. The part.

Dad's big day was drawing near
He practiced round the clock
Cut back on fags and beer
And jogged around the block

Friends we never knew we had
Came knocking at the door
We got good luck cards from family
Who we'd never met before

Locals down the Crown and Goose
Got right behind our dad
They were sick of seeing Wapping lose
He was the best chance that they had

Dad woke me up
Then we woke up Mum
The waiting was over
Dad's big day had come

We took a train to Nottingham
The Heart of the Midlands the club was named
And we took a seat among the crowd
That had come to see the game

Ron, Big Ronnie, undisputed Pub-King of Cheam
Sank his pint, rose up from the bar
And gazed upon the mayhem

He had his entourage with him
From the underworld
Harry and Mad Michael Franks
And a throng of others followers
Including a chat show host, a soap actor
And a couple of young stars from West Ham
Ron had established himself as a bit of a boy

Now, we were told,
As a matter of course he loves to turn up early
And always with his better half
Shirley

It was a superstition of sorts.

I watched him prowl the length of the back bar.

Eyes wide. Fixed.

Dad was back-stage
Safe in the comparative calm of the player's bar
When I popped through to get him
We left for the practice board

He threw a few looseners
Neither of us spoke
Didn't keep the score
No point no more

I went back to sit with Mum
Walking through a fog of *eau de cologne* and smoke
Past the slop of lager and the reek of bitter

Mum was sat with her sister, with me
A family gathering of three

The MC took the stage and an almighty hush descended

Black tie, shaved head
White shirt, dickie bow
He wore his head up high
Kept his voice down low
Clean cut. Sharp
Shoulders wide
Patience thin
The bobby dazzling lights
Glistened off his chin
A shave so close you wonder
How he kept hold of his skin
You could smell his Brut '33

From off the TV
But you wouldn't rub it in

Cameras go live in five
Four
Three
Two

(Silent count on one)

LADIES AND GENTLEMEN
ARE YOU READY?

Crowd go wild.

THEN THE VERY BEST OF ORDER PLEASE.
LETS! PLAY! DARTS!

RON TO THROW FIRST
GAME ON

Ron 60, 20, 60
140 from 501 leaves 361

Dad 60, 60, 5
125 from 501 leaves 376

Ron 60, 60, 40,
Down to 201

Dad 60, 20, 60
Back on 236

Ron 60, 57 –
(dropped down for treble 19, takes off the one.
Good cover.
That's a treble leaves him on 24. Double 12. His favourite
finish.)

Dad 60, 1, 20

Way back.
Failed to pressurise the shot

Ron you require 24

Game shot and the first leg.

Cool as you like
Steady
First leg to Big Ron
Dad yet to get off the mark

SECOND LEG. BOBBY TO THROW FIRST
GAME ON.

Dad 60, 40, 20

Ron, 60, 20, 60

Dad 60, 20, 20

Ron 60, 20, 20

Dad 60, 20, 40
Leaves him on 161
That's a finish and Ron's way back

Ron 60, 20, 20

BOBBY YOU REQUIRE 161

Come on dad
Lets get off the mark
60, leaves 101
Treble 17's the shot
Got it –
Leaves the bull for the second leg?
Bull?
Oooh. Close. 16 I think. Leaves 34
Double 17
– But here comes Ron

And Ron was fire.

GAME SHOT. THAT'S THE SECOND LEG
16, Double 8
And that's the third leg

Ron Ron Ron Ron Ron Ron Ron Ron Ron

It was ugly

Ron was bullying him
Beating him up bad

And I hated Big Ron
For doing that to Dad.

Ron 60, 60, 60
180

Double 9,
That's game shot

Treble 17, Bull
Game shot and the third leg,

Ron Ron Ron Ron Ron Ron Ron Ron Ron Ron

Dad was looking old up there
His face was almost white
He seemed to whither on the stage
His dreams fading into night

Ron Ron Ron Ron Ron

Double 12 – that's Game Shot
Fifth leg

Dad had lost his focus,
He looked around the crowd

Then, in the midst of his despair
He caught sight of a little gathering
That he didn't know was there
But there they were. Three groups of five
All wearing joke shop wigs
Big blonde shocks of flowing locks
And pink gold matching shirts
Inscribed upon them – Bobby Tops
Real live fans and these were his first
He looked around the room
more of his fans standing at the bar

They'd made the trip from Wapping
Which to Nottingham's quite far
Everywhere he looked he saw others,
two, three, then four
Their banners made it clear why they were here
Put simply. He weren't alone no more

It went unnoticed by Big Ron
But in Dad
Deep down inside
It stirred up pride
Enough to spur him on
He later told me blow by blow
Relived every shot
He wanted me to know, you see
To know the bloody lot

I remember what I saw of course
Don't forget that I was there
But to hear it is another thing
The two just don't compare

So, Dad pulled himself up tall
And won four on the run
Doesn't matter which way you slice it
The comeback had begun

The colour was back in his face
In his step a spring
He played for pride of place
And he didn't miss a thing.

Ton 40s coming thick and fast
Thick and fast indeed
He stuck with double nine
And in double time
He'd knocked off Big Ron's lead
Double nine –
Got it
Got it
The match was poised at five legs all

The deciding leg for the match
Game on

The MC took the mike
He tried to calm the crowd
But they were going mad by now
So he turned the mike up loud

LADIES AND GENTLEMEN
THE VERY BEST OF ORDER
AND IN THE INTERESTS OF BOTH PLAYERS
NO CALLING OUT ON THE SHOT

Ron to throw first

Now – I know what's coming next
And what came next changed us all forever
But I didn't know that at the time
How could I? We never do. Never

We're back into the match

And it's Ron to throw first

Only the MC's having words
And now Big Ron's left the stage
Dad's left up there hanging
For what felt like a blooming age

It's not on. Not fair
I felt like he could melt up there
Marooned under the lights – the glare

Finally Dad does the right thing too and
Heads off-stage. It's a key leg after all

Got to keep cool

Seconds tick over.

Then minutes.

Still no sign of Big Ron
Then, eventually he rolls back on

Fresh – up for it
Soon after – Dad

Game on

Ron's got the first throw
All he's got to do
is hold himself together
and he's favourite to go through

But funny things can happen
When it comes to pressure darts
And Dad was fit and up for it
And in with every chance

If he could just pressure the shot
Let Ronnie know he was there

Ron, 60, 60
Camera zooms in
20
140

Good start

Dad 60, 60, 20
140

Level pegging
Neck and neck

Ron, 60, 60, 60
180

What a time for a maximum
Leaves 181
Could be a ten dart finish

Back comes Dad
60, 20, 6– ooh
That's unlucky
What a time to get
A bounce out
He's way back on 281

Ron, 60, 20, 12
92 leaves him 89
Nice out shot

Dad. Has to pressurise
60, now needs…that's double 12
And dropping down for 17s?
What's he playing at?
That's left a tough out shot

Now surely, for the match – Big Ron

RON YOU REQUIRE 89

Could go treble 20,
5 double 12
Got options
Double 16, single 7 for bull?

How you feeling?

Treble 20

Then a 13

Leaves 16.
Double eight for the match
Wrong bed!
Double 16
Bust
Back to 89

Dad's in with a shot
But this is a big ask
146. Needs a treble
Must start with a treble.

BOBBY YOU REQUIRE 146

Treble 20 treble 20 double 13's the shot
Here goes
Single 3?
Treble 14?

That's an odd choice
He can't finish
Single 19
Leaves him on 82
Don't understand that

The smile on Mad Michael Franks face

The same smile I saw years later
On the inside –

But more on that later

RON. YOU REQUIRE 89

Could go treble 17 (51'd leave 38)
Single 2 for double 18
He could stay up on the 20s for treble 5
Could be the shot
It'd leave him 24
Check from 89 on double 12
Yes, he's been that way before

Treble 15
Could go single 10 for double 17
There's the single –
now
for the match
One dart
Double Top

Release

Through the air
Shuffling like some minute bird
Spiralling slow
Spinning fast
Dipping
Drilling in towards its target
Bronze alloy balanced weight
Pockmarked and roughed for grip
The feathered tail

Blue, white
Sky-like

On their feet in the Heart of the Midlands
All eyes on the board

Pause.

Ron's done it.

That's double top.

He's got the match.

Pause.

At the time I didn't know the impact it would have on my life
But from that shot on…nothing would ever be the same
It led to a life of crime
Of hustle and bustle and doing time
And all 'cos of one stupid, poxy little dart
But Dad lost and the cost tore him apart
And that broke my heart

After the match Big Ron blanked him at the bar
Following Monday he tells everyone
That my old man won't get far
'Lacks the bottle on the big shot,
Nice bloke, but prone to choke
When there's a chance to kill it off'

There was no way back from there for Dad
His only chance at playing pro-darts
Was the one he'd only just had

He made a few more attempts to qualify
But he didn't hang around that long
Others had come on, he'd lost his form
And he knew his chance had gone

Well – Dad sat slumped in his chair
Mum was unhappy and so was I
He was back on fags and beers
And the days just passed him by

I couldn't bear to stay at home
It reeked of that defeat
And mum left crying on her own
And dad struggling to make ends meet

Day I turned 18 I wanted out
Mum begged me not to go
But I couldn't stay another day
I didn't want to know

All the excuses Dad had made
Spent his evenings down the boozer
Talking crap about this and that
like any other loser

Don't be hard on him son
He tried his best, gave it his all
I didn't want to shout at Mum
I might say something cruel

Did his best? He's given up
I don't want to end up like that
Like what? Says Mum that's your Dad
He gave you everything you had
He'd do anything for you
Done things for you; you never knew
He don't talk about it all, just his way
So you be careful what you say

'He's given up mum, he's left it to you
And all 'cos he couldn't win
I'll never end up like that'
'Like What?' 'Like him'

'Him?' You watch your mouth says Mum
There's plenty there that you don't know
Yeah – well I know enough. Enough for what?
Enough to want to go

'Him? Him?' That's your father you're talking about
If only you knew the half of it – if only you knew

'Knew what?' I go 'The truth you silly sod, she said
'He threw that bloody match. He threw that match – for you.'

Turns out Dad didn't lose…it was fixed.

To bookies money's all that matters
Cash comes in and they farm it out
5 grand a horse, it's a matter of course
It's win-win if you got the clout
And these boys don't fuck about

They protect their bets with nasty threats
It goes on every week
Cleaning money
That smells a bit of funny
Before it starts to reek
And there's kids out there
Who just don't care
And so the price of life is cheap
A screwdriver and a fiver
And they'd do you in their sleep

They hadn't bothered with Dad at first 'cos he was a rank
outsider. Only he was looking a bit tasty up there and could
have nicked it. He could have interfered with things. He was
making a nuisance of himself. They had it that Ron would go
down 3 to 1 to Kenth Ohlsson in the quarters. A lot of money
riding on it and Dad was getting on their tits. They got to him
when he followed Ron off-stage. He was told to throw the
match if he ever wanted to see his son again.
The whole fucking thing was a stitch up.
The whole fucking thing was a stitch up.
The whole fucking thing. Was a stitch up.

And I weren't having it.
Not now I knew what went on
And that's why. Ten years later.
I urged my Dad to go and find Big Ron.

Ron had never gone on to lift the crown
But he made a real fist of being a pro

So much so that by 1988
He'd retired, had a family and bought a pub in Bow

So.

Ten years on
We're walking to the pub
The Crown and Anchor
Ronnie's
We don't talk
There was nothing more to say
Dad was out to prove a point

We get to the boozer…

Crumbling bricks, rain stained, blue smoke
A charmless pub by any standards
It was tired. Feeling its age
A bit like Dad

I hold open the door. In we go.

The features were original. Victorian windows distorted and
discoloured. All brass and mirrors. Stray chairs and moth-eaten
booths. Dark. The punters looked every inch as empty as the
glasses Ron was collecting from the tables. Every bit as burnt
out as the fag ends that lined the ashtrays on the bar.

Then I see Pat in the corner. He's with Flannagan. A bare
knuckle boxer. The size of him. The size of his neck.

We got ourselves a drink

Dad sits down

They stare at Dad
Dad stares back

Pause.

The bell rang time

We did not leave

Then the shutters came down. Curtains drawn

Lock in

Those that weren't waiting to play were here to watch. Ron's
game of killer was famous in Bow. And a lot of money would
change hands in side bets.

The stage. Was set. For Killer.

A quid a head the stake
The pot went round
To collect each pound
Only there was some mistake

Hello? What's this? 15 players
But only 14 quid
They launched a quick enquiry
And the blame was put on Sid

'I pay my dues' he argued
Understandably upset
'I've played every year
Since coming here
And I ain't ducked a payment yet'

'Well, someone's trying it on all right
We're short to the tune of a quid'

Mickey Mick turns on Knuckle Jim
And Jimmy's no one's mug
He'd paid his stake, and didn't take
To being hassled by this thug

Alfie Bates butted in
His rasping voice pickled in gin
'Don't blame Alf for the missing quid
He was the first to stick his in.'

'Then who's the bloody stowaway?'
Things were shaping up that night
There was something in the air
And the only thing that stopped a fight
Was Dad getting out of his chair

'Oi. It's my name up there
And no. I haven't paid my fare
This may sound funny
But I'll keep my money
till I'm beaten fair and square'

Silence.
There was a stranger in their bar.

'All right.' Says Ron. 'Let him play.'

So round and round the players go
Round and round the clock
From 1 to 20 fifteen players
Each 3 lives. One shot
Each playing for the pot
14 golden coins therein
They glistened and they gleamed
But there was more at stake
Than the money they'd make
There was more to all than this it seemed

There was Little Lil,
Then Paddy Gray
Then Joe, then Russian Vlad
Then Jim the Knuckle,
Then Sneaky Sid
and after Ron came Dad
Yep. After Ron
Came Dad

Round and round the players go
Round and round they went
Like a slow revolve of stiff resolve
And each dart thrown was meant

Round one did for Mac and Dave
Round three saw off Johnny Day
Round four claimed three more
Now there's only six left to play

Joe missed, but Lil hit her treble 14

'Well done Lil' cried her old man Joe
But she missed her nine
As did Vlad next time
Now there's only three left to throw

Jim, Ron and Dad

Jim knuckled down
An almighty frown
One last shot
If he wants to stop
Ron from lifting the crown
He threw – hard/fast
But needed it a fraction higher
'Bad luck there Jim,' shouts Paddy
'You bent the fucking wire'

Two men left
Sudden death
Dad and Ron
Game on

Ron turned to Dad

'I remember you'

Dad didn't flinch, just fixed him with a stare
'I'd like to see you beat me now it's fair and square'

You could have cut the air in the pub that night
The locals huddled round
'Five grand says I can take you,' said Dad
Ron silently looked round

'Ten,' Ron goes. 'Ten grand and you're on.'
It had taken Dad years to scrimp the five
Now he needs ten to bury Ron

'I can't do it' he says
'Five's all I've got. I'm not a bank'
'I'll cover you' says a voice from the back
The voice of Mad Michael Franks

Closest to the bull then.

Dad looks edgy, shuffling on his feet
Ron is calm and cocky
My heart's pounding. I can hear it beat
as he goes to toe the oche

'Go on Ron. Go on now.
Come on Ron. Come on Ronnie'

Outside of the bull. Close.
But outside.

Dad's got his chance

Up steps Dad.

Silence.

Hand shaking like foil, heart jumping
You could hear a pin
Eyes narrow, furrowed brow
Light glimmering off his rings
Big Ron behind, can't look, I can't look
I saw my old man's hand
It shook

Release
Through the air
Shuffling like some minute bird
Spiralling slow
Spinning fast
Dipping
Drilling in towards its target
Bronze alloy balanced weight
Pockmarked and roughed for grip
The feathered tail
Blue, white
Sky-like

On their feet in the heart of the East End
All eyes on the board

No. Not even close.

Ron retained his crown
He took the ten grand
And the fifteen quid

Dad never recovered

He'd lost to Ron once and for all
And saddled with the debt to Michael Franks
He sat slumped in his chair
And stared at the box for years

Make matters worse he went on to watch
Big Ron make a comeback and get
All the way to the final; he didn't win but
He went up to collect his nice fat
Runner's-up check on TV
And he was flushed with joy
As Shirley rushed the stage with their
Brand new baby boy – Lee

See even though he'd lost he'd won
They had three little girls and now he had a son

Big Ron's life was complete

He didn't need the money –
He could have called off the debt
But he screwed Dad for every last penny
All from some sleazy back-room beer-stained bet

Dad couldn't keep up with the interest

Maybe he was ashamed
maybe he couldn't take the pressure
just couldn't see a way out…

His body was cold to the touch when
Mum found him in the garage…
He'd unplugged the gas from the heater
And locked himself in…

Dad – took his own life…

Now it was just me and Mum.

I got saddled with the remainder of Dad's debt.

Couldn't pay it so I was made to work for Harry –

Harry was one of Frank's lot
Collecting debts from dodgy bets
And skimming off the top

And I was mopping up after him
Clearing up all his crap
What I was for, was his man on the door
Who could step in with a bit of a slap

But – at all costs I would avoid violence
Biggest weapon I would pull was silence…

Did I occasionally drive splinters
Down the finger nails of cocky little
Bastards who thought they'd fleece a few quid?
'Course I didn't, 'course I did

Depends who you ask…

I was a bit tasty, see
I was tough, I had clout
But truth is it just wasn't me
I'd had enough, I wanted out

And so I made my biggest mistake yet,
I'd had a couple of wins on the horses
And thought I could gamble my way out of the debt

You know you're going to lose
But you think you're going to win
Your mind tricks you
It lures you in

I used Harry's money…
money I'd collected from the debts

I had his 20 grand in my hand
And put it all on bets

Lost the lot.
Now what?

I can't leg it. He'll get to Mum
I can't believe the mess I'm in.
Can't believe what I've done

I know Harry. He's a killer
He can kill
Part of me thinks he won't
And part of me thinks he will

I need twenty grand – today

I empty my wallet, borrow what I can
From friends and mum
Scaring them to death I am – they sense my fear
I tell 'em not to worry, get out in a hurry
But twenty grand… I'm nowhere near

Who can can I turn to? Who can I turn to?

Then I remember – Pat.

He's a trainer by profession but he's as bent as they come.

If there's a fix – he's on it. He knows when a favourite is
going to blow up. Or when a jockey's been told to ride round
tenderly.

He's given me a bunch of tips in the last year or two and
they've all come in. Every last one.

I find him in Mulligans. He's with some gypsies. Willis, Cobb
and Flanagan.

And they've flogged him the back end of an Irish mare. And I
want in. It's my ticket out.

I stand 'em all a drink and I get myself two. Doubles.

I knew what Pat wanted to hear. So I said it.

'Pat. Please.'

Two grand buys me a stake in Snuggles. The racehorse he part-owns with the gypsies. And Snuggles runs today at 4:45. There's a large purse. Enough to be split five ways.

Not only will I have the money for Harry but I'll have enough to pay off the debt to Franks as well.

At last... Mum and me...
We'll be free.

And I'll go straight. Get on with my life.

I get to the racecourse. Look up at the starter's guide.
What's this? Snuggles – way out a 100 to 1

I move over to the hospitality tent
And I'm standing about looking round
Where is everyone?

I've done my nuts on a rank outsider.
No sign of the gypsies or Pat

Out come the horses.
Into the enclosure.
Then, towards the back – Snuggles

Do me a favour?
Looks like a bleeding donkey
And I got talked into part-ownership
I part-own that piece of shit

Ladies day
Long flowing dresses
Hats
Brims, butterflies – pink gin
Elegance

Few spots of rain

Turf accountants winding up
Princess of Monaco
Looking through binoculars

Everyone's ready
Poised

Hand on my shoulder. It's Pat.

'You okay son?'
'What do you think? She's a bloody no-hoper.'
'A bit of money's come in now'

I look up to the starter's guide. He's right. She's come in from
100 to 66. Still, 66 I won't hold my breath.

'Pat, is she going to win?'
'Well, we could do with some rain.'
'For fuck's sake Pat. Has this race been rigged or what?'
'It has, aye. But…'
'But what?'

Bang

They're off

Sudden move
Into stride
Hooves thundering
Big pack, not split
Too tight, too together
One big horse
Big jump coming up
Get up – too early

Clash – most over
Two fallers
Are we down? Are we down?
No. Lost Captain Dandy and Sole Survivor

Look about.
Princess of Monaco
And there's the gypsies
Do they know something?
What do they know?

Race not found its rhythm

Boxed in all of 'em
Tight as a pack but on they go

Fence Two
And it's a bastard

'Easy now Kieran. Stay on it. Stay on it.'

Mayhem all around
Thunder of hooves
Lashing rain

'Get up Kieran. Get up'

Done. Well timed. Well jumped.

Pardon What, Mantilla, Lady of the Lamp, Lucky Leader
Classified, Dutch Gold, Parlight, Bustling Rio, Midnight Creek

Where are they?
Where the fuck?
Where the fuck are they?

Nowhere.
Not even in the next bloody lot

Royal Windmill, King of Peru, Shotgun Willy, Spot the
Difference
Sudden Shock, Sir Frosty, Last Option, Midnight Gunner,
Roberty Bob

Forget it
Forget it!

Time for plan B.
Only what is plan B?

Look around
There's Harry.
And Cherry

Beautiful woman. Truth is – he doesn't deserve her.
Knocks her about. He ought to treat her better.

Maybe then she wouldn't have a thing for me.

She made it clear first time I ever met her

Harry, Cherry and me were in a bar. They both ask for a vodka martini and I get myself a whisky and coke. Then Cherry decides she'd now rather have a whisky and coke. I thought you wanted a vodka martini I said. Well, I made a mistake she says. I'd now like a whisky and coke. I think you should stick with vodka martini, don't you. No, I don't, she goes. You get me a whisky and coke. I didn't. I know which side my bread's buttered. Least I thought I did.

'Shit, mind yourself Kieran!'

Sudden Shock tangling with Mantilla at ten
Big fence rears up after Palmer's Turn
4 foot by 10 then 5 by 9

King of Peru pulls up
Shotgun Willy unseats rider

Last Option – gone
Classified – gone
Lady of the Lamp, Carryonharry,
Innox, Big Brown Bear
Gone, gone, gone, gone

Where are we?
Are we still there?

All of them onto 12
Death track. Muddying up
Rain sapping 'em. Soft ground
Chopping in. Turfing up.
Horses knackered – spent
Given it all

Who's left?
Who's got what?
Who's got what left?

Four fences out
Now it matters

Now it matters
Now it counts

Up onto 13

'Hold your line Kieran. Hold your line.'

Lucky Leader, Parlight, Bustling Rio, Midnight Creek, Master
Pa, Smarter Charter, Don Royale, Ajar, Prancing Blade,
Shotgun Willy, Snuggles, Spot the Difference, Classified

We're in this
We're in this
We're fucking in it

Moral Support, Midnight Gunner, Roberty Bob
All coming up to 14

'Veer in Kieran. That's it. That's it. That's it Snuggles.

Kick on now, kick on, kick on'

Three fences out

Picking it up
Picking it up
A late charge

Past Winter Whisper and Master Pa
And Blushing Groom and Alaska
Past Ajar and Prancing Blade
Past Don Royale and Bonus Maid

Two fences out

Come on
Come on Kieran
Come on
Come on
Come on Snuggles
Come on
Come on
Come on you cunts!

Pause.

In the end it came down to a two horse race. Snuggles and Parlight battling it out. Parlight had more strength in the end and Snuggles seemed to hit the wall, slowing up she mistimed a jump. Nasty fall.

'Don't like the look of that,' says Pat. 'Don't like the look of that at all.'

Race was over. Plan B. Still haven't got a plan B.

I follow Pat, asking what went wrong but he was more concerned about Kieran and Snuggles. We run onto the course.

If a horse is injured they'll take it away in a horse box. If the fall was heavy and the damage severe, then they erect a screen around the horse and do what's necessary on the spot.

The vet confirmed everyone's fears:
'It's a break'

The racing community are pretty good at not hearing the shot. People only hear what they want to hear.

That's why I couldn't reason with Harry.

It's important that the gun's discreet.

Last thing you want to do is spook the horse.

In this case it was a snub-nosed revolver

There are two ways to shoot the horse

The right way and the wrong way

The right way is to aim straight between the eyes. Point down slightly. And shoot through the skull, through the brain and onto the top of the spinal column. Aim it right and one shot's all you need.

Get it wrong and it can take two or even three shots, maybe more. Now the horse will be in a lot of pain…

I tell the vet I'll do this myself. He says no. Fuck it. I grab the gun. Aim as I was told. Right between the eyes. Bang. One shot. Done the trick. I'd taken out Pat. Knee-capped the fucker.

Well, I'd worked it out. Pat was working for Harry. So were the gypsies, the bookies, the accountants. Everywhere I turn it's Harry, Harry, Harry, Harry. Pat knew that Parlight had to win. I rock up desperate earlier and he pretends to help me out. Really, he sees an opportunity to offload his stake in a horse he knows is going down.

Known him all my life and he sells me out for a few grand

Fuck him. Fuck him.

Vet gets up and I knock him back down

Half of me wants to get the fuck out

But Snuggles is in a lot of pain and I want to put her out of it

Bang.

There's blood everywhere and she's shitting herself and pissing herself and the stench… I just want to get the fuck out but I can't. Not yet. She's still in pain and I can't have that. She's done nothing wrong. Tried her fucking heart out. And such a sad, sad look in her big black eyes. I knew how she felt.

Bang. Bang.

Fuck it. I've to get out of here. Fast.

Now I'm fucked. Well and truly… I've lost Harry's money …

Hold it together now. Hold it together and think fast. Mustn't let Harry get hold of me.

I've got seconds. If that. My only chance is to stay clear of him for long enough to get myself nicked. Maybe I can rat on him. Strike a deal. If they'll believe me. I don't know. I don't know. I'm fucked.

I step out from behind the screen and twat a jockey holding onto Roberty Bob. Nothing personal. Just a slap so I can hop on the horse.

Hop on. Who am I kidding? You ever tried getting on a racehorse without a fucking step ladder? Well try it when your life depends on it.

Bit of a struggle but I'm up.

And once I'm on we're off. He goes. Just fucking goes.

I'm hanging on for dear life. See the sky swirl, punters one way, a forest the other. Smell of wet grass. Clean air.

We're now galloping and I don't know where to – all I'm trying to do is stay on long enough to get arrested. That's my plan. But it's not easy. Horse is going nuts. Then all of a sudden it makes up its mind where it's going. It hits its stride. And we're off

Pounding, pounding
Pounding, pounding

Oh no…fuck me we're heading straight for hospitality.

Screams, shouts, smashing of glass, people running trying to get out the way. Mayhem. Total pandemonium. I'm flung off and land in the corner of the tent. I see a tray of canapés turned up. I look in the tray to check my reflection.

Fucking state of me. Arms cut to ribbons. Legs slashed to bits. And you could get twins through the gash above my eye.

Everything goes into slow motion. I can see people shouting but can't hear the words. I think I can hear a police siren. Come on boys. Chop, chop.

   Pause.

I wake up slowly. From the inside out. Feel my heart beating first. Then voices. Not many. And not cops. Where am I?

I try to move but can't.

Shadows flicker.

A light flashing in my eyes
One at a time

Hospital maybe. No I look around.

I'm in a barn.

I adjust to the light and focus on the face that's staring at me

It's Harry. He explains that I've been injected with a controlled amount of ACP. A muscle relaxant.

Relaxed? I couldn't fucking move. I got tunnel vision. Can't see past Harry. Maybe I never could.

Harry spoke…

'Where's my money?'

'Harry listen –'

'Shut it you useless cunt. I looked after you. I bought the debt, bought you off Franks. I said, leave him Michael, he's a boy, I said. I'll use him, I'll put him out to work. Do with a pair of hands. I gave you a chance. I gave you things. A life. Gave you a life, and money. I gave you money. And this is how you repay me. Liberty. Bleeding liberty.'

Then he loses it.

'You're nothing, all you are. Nothing, nothing, nothing, nothing, nothing, nothing. Fuck all is all you are. Fuck all. Don't you fucking get it?'

'Please Harry, I –'

'Shut it – !'

I can see his face but it's changing shape like I'm looking at him through a kaleidoscope. ACP is strong stuff. I'm starting to trip my nuts off. And I can't hear his words now. Can't even keep focused on anything by now. Keep seeing Snuggles, the look in her big sad eyes. I'm walking up a dark street as a kid.

In a duffel coat and I can smell horse chestnuts burning and I realise that this is the first time I've remembered it. I thought of a garden sprinkler in a shed that never used to work and how it got dusty in a shed. I remembered being on a bus with my mum, she'd just bought me a new set of darts with Popeye flights on them. I remember standing on a box so I could reach the pool table. I remember being late to the pictures with Laura, my first girlfriend, we got lost, but she didn't mind and she was so beautiful that nothing seemed to matter. I come round a bit. I see –

Harry looking into my eyes. Gun at my head. Staring into my brain. This is an execution. I try not to think about it. I try not to think at all. I look down…

The stone cold floor, the damp stinking bricks, the crumbling fucking paint. The last fucking shitty things I'd ever fucking see.

Bang.

I look up. Can't feel anything. I'm still here. I'm still here. I look round.

Harry's brains all over the show. Cherry shaking. Gun in her hand.

'Harry doesn't own us anymore.' That's all she says.

I can't believe I'm alive. I'm too happy to think. But I have to. For Cherry.

'Get out,' I say. 'Thank you. Thank you but – go. Leave the gun and go. Just go.'

'What you going to do?'

'Go, just go. Please. Before anyone comes.'

Cops rolled up and I did the time for Cherry
Least I could do after what she did for me
I pleaded self-defense
And the judge sat
on the fence

They gave me 15 – but after nine

I'd be…well, I say free…

But you never really leave prison

I kept myself fit, and I exercised my mind
I'd do press-ups and sit-ups by the bed
Then I'd lie on it and read
Yes, I read and I read and I read

Poems as well
I got to quite like them

Keats, Browning, Hopkins, Tennyson

Lovely stuff
once you get into it all – it's a whole new world
I read a different one every day
It'd make the walls disappear –
Make 'em go away

We had people come in and talk about them
Lecturers
Roddy and Jill – nice people – straight but
Still – they was okay – put 'emselves out
to teach you stuff –
give you a sense of what's it all about

But still – you can't read all the fucking time –

I was hoping the exams would help with my parole
But they helped me with more –

As I say – they helped to keep sane

You can go mad inside
As prisoners know full well
You can go nuts over nothing
And smash up your cell
Make no mistake.
It is hell. It is hell

And the thing that's worst

Hits you first
And that's the bleeding smell
Putrid

You can almost taste the sweat
Which mingles in with piss and shit
And you wait all day for food
But it's so awful you don't touch it
Once it's there

And it's boring, so bloody boring
You just don't know what to do
So you do nothing, 'cos doing nothing's
Better than nothing at all
And you pace up and down
with your mind going round
about ways to get over the wall

and it's the sounds. It's the sounds
the jangle of keys as the guards do the rounds
and you find new ways
to chalk off the days
till there are no more ways to be found

And it's the screams and the shouts
and the slamming of doors
and the bare knuckle bouts
and the underground tours
which are led by the screws
to a solitary cell
where when tanked up on booze
they kick six shades of hell
out of some poor bloke
who spoke out of turn
or who lit up a smoke
'cos he wanted to burn
His way out of his piss shitting cell
That papers call prison
And prisoners call hell
And it's all very well

They can do what they like
'cos who can you tell
in the middle of the night
that the screws came in
and tore you to bits
and picked up a bucket
chock-full of your shit
and smeared it all over the walls

but who'll ever know
well, no one at all.

And it's the screams
It's the screams
From the paranoid psychos
And their paranoid dreams

And it's the feel of the place
With it's cold steel bars
And it's grey dank walls
Which keep you so bloody far
From the life you once knew
That continues outside
And when glimpsed from the window
Brings tears for the years
You'll be spending inside

But you can't show the bastards they're getting you down
And you can't show the bastards you're getting upset
And you can't and you don't and you don't 'cos you won't
Want the bastards to see any weaknesses yet.

Don't stop 'em for trying though…

2465 – this – 2465 – that…

On and on…banging on your door
They may as well be banging on your skull

But you're there and that's that
No choice

It becomes your life

Though you dream of getting out

You serve out the time
You serve out the time
You serve out the time

And you get used to it

And you develop habits

Ever wondered why so many villains on the street talk out the
corner of their mouths?

Habit from prison where you're not allowed to talk
So you learn to talk without getting caught

'Don't turn round.'

Blimey.

It's Alf. Alfie Bates.
One of my old man's mates

'You're Bobby's boy ain't you?'
It's him all right.
'Don't say nothing son. Say nothing to no one.
Nothing at all.'
'But this time next week a few of us are going over the wall.'

Well blow me –

I was made up – fuck parole
I'm getting out on my own terms
I sat around with my feet up
I walked with a roll

I'm not saying I was sure I'd make it
I wasn't. Couldn't be. 'Course not. No.
But I was just happy to be trying
Just glad to be having a go

Next few days we put it all together
Each of us have our part to play

Mine was to cause a scene

Then a van'll come in and take me off to Broadmoor. Only I won't end up in Broadmoor. 'Cos Range Rover number one will come out the bushes and smash the fucking prison van into a ditch at 40 miles an hour. Range Rover number two takes me home.

I'll keep a low profile for a while
Change of name
See my Mum straight and then who knows?
There's options...
Maybe a pub or a bar in Spain
That's the plan...
And we can do this
And we know we can

12:45 – Lunch
And I move to the front of the queue

2645. Line! Back of! Now!
Eh?
You heard. Back. Now.
'You bastard screw.'
'What did you say?'
'Nothing'
'Did you call me a bastard?'

So now I'm in control
I walk slowly to the back of the queue
Like I'm supposed to do
It's all part of my role

I don't say anything

I just smash my fucking tray across the silly bastard's face
Again and again and again

From nowhere it kicks off

Other inmates are in on it and they turn over a table

Chair lock a door

We get up on our feet. Chanting and stamping

'Go! Go! Go! Go! Go! Go! Go! Go!'

Meanwhile Alf has got his boys nearby…
Two range Rovers on the A232

I rip up chairs
Start a fire
Block off the stairs

Screws panic at times like this
The alarm goes off

I make it clear I'm the ringleader

Get up on a table, chair leg in hand
And taunt the screws in their riot gear

'Come on then. Let's have you! Have a pop! Have a fucking
pop! Let's fucking go!'

The screws close in – raining in blows

It was very bright. Strange colours.

Dad didn't look much older
And he seemed jolly, like the old days
Maybe he was just happy to see me
We were on a walk – just a walk

It was nice to be with him again
We talked about our trips to Brighton
We liked them, with Mum
Some egg and cress sandwiches,
a hot flask, pebbled beach below
walking along the pier…the old one
Nice times…simple

I knew Dad had something on his mind.

'It weren't like what you think son. Ask 'em what really
happened. You should know the truth.'

I turned round to say something –

But he'd turned into someone else

A door that I didn't know was there opens
Light floods in

'Bye son.'

'Dad?'

I spun round but there was nothing. Just a feeling of falling

I'd received a fatal blow in the riot

Doctors worked through the night

But I was pronounced dead at 2:19 am

I was revived at 2:21 am

Somehow they brought me back to life

I'd missed the jail break. I wondered if Alf had made it.

Still at least I was alive.

I was blamed for starting the riot and got given another five.
Back to prison life. More years of the same old

Same old, same old

Day after day after day....

Month on month...

Years....

Then Tuesday morning and I'm on my way to slop out only
I'm not allowed to

That was the first sign that something was up
Then it turned out that we were being held over for some
reason.
Not allowed in the yard till after lunch

Something was up...
Gossip went round...
But no one knew what was going down

We knew it was something though
It wasn't just the break in routine
It was the unfamiliar atmosphere

The day just had a different rhythm

Then we learnt that we had a new arrival

And not just any old new arrival either

The prison gates were mobbed
Press were in a frenzy

The screws were apprehensive
The governor was tense

And then it all came clear
Suddenly it all made sense

They'd got him.
They'd bloody got him

Mad Michael Franks

Big catch for the old Bill...

He'd been wanted for 25 years

The paparazzi left disappointed

He'd been ghosted in from Parkhurst
They'd kept him out the glare
And for the first few weeks
It was like he wasn't even there

But he was

Fancy seeing you in here?
He gave me one of his looks
He'd got a soft job in the library
Just sorting out the books

'Am I supposed to know who you are?'
He knew all right. This was a game.
He'd blanked me but then slipped up
When he called me by my name

He looked away
But I hadn't finished
I had things to say

'You're nothing now Franks. Nothing in here'
That got his attention. I met his stare
'Who do you think you're talking to?'
'I'm talking to you, you piece of shit.
You're nothing in here Franks.
And you were nothing out there'

That's when I learnt the truth
The truth about my Dad
He didn't kill himself,
They just made it look as though he had

Well, I made a vow that day
A vow I later made to Mum
That Michael Franks and Ron
Would pay for what they done

I swore that day that come what may
I would right the wrong
I'd do Mad Michael Franks
And then I'd do Big Ron

'He got a bit mouthy,' says Franks
'Told us he weren't going to pay
And when people owe us money
We don't let 'em get away'
I'll get you Franks.
I'll get you if it's the last thing I ever do
To me you're just a piece of shit
That needs scraping off my shoe

Franks smiles, looks over and nods
and from nowhere a bastard
screw jumps me

From that day on my life inside is...
Not a lot of fun.

But thinking of Cherry kept me going
As did visits. From my Mum

I don't want to talk too much about –
When I told her what happened well…
It upset me to see her upset.
I was upset too but
I hate to upset my Mum
I asked her not to visit but she did
She wanted to see her son

One of the boys would bring her in
Knuckle Jim and she'd have a gift
for me from Honest Alf
The boys made sure she was okay
And by the way – you now know
That Alf got out

And good luck to him

My mum would give me little presents
Nothing much else she can do
A bar of soap, some phone cards and fags
And a bottle of scotch – some hope
The screw nicked all the nice stuff
Though he let me keep the soap

Prison is all about routine
Lights out
Recreation
Lunch
Slopping out
Shower – twice a week

They strip search us on the way in

I stayed in there for ages…
Got the soap worked into a lather

The soap was soft and pliable
And very carefully made

It crumbled in my hand
To reveal a nice, sharp blade

The rest was easy for me
I knew what to do next…
I knew who I had to see
'Hello Franks. It's me.'

The look in Mad Michael Franks' eye
As he saw the piece of steel glisten
He tried to shout
But nothing came out
And anyway –
there was no one who would listen

'You think you're untouchable
Well, not in here you ain't'
I cut off his cock and split his bollocks
And watched the bastard faint

Mad Michael Franks, all that money and power
And there he was now – left
To be chopped down in a group shower
Where he slowly bled to death

By the time Franks had slid
down the wall
I'd gone
Towelled off fast
And walked straight past
The on-duty screw
No one knew
'Cos no one saw fuck all

I lit up a fag and sat on my bed
Looked out the bars

The sky was blood red
And a couple of seagulls screamed
overhead

Part one had been done
Next in line was Ron
And I was due my release
And feeling at peace
because I was
keeping my vow to Mum
I lay on my bed
And tried not to think
about what I'd become

The gates opened.
'See you soon,' says the screw
'You're the one still here mate,
And I'm off – so fuck you.'

The first thing that struck me
On the outside was the smells
Perfume, freshly cut grass,
And the space – all that space
I sat down on a bench in a daze
I had to think it out, find ways
Of…well…coping…
There were still things I had to face

I wasn't quite free
Never would be till I'd done Big Ron
Only then could I think about me
Only then could I move on

It didn't take long before
I got back to where I was
I picked up where I left off
And it was easy for me because

Alf and Knuckle Jim
Had got hold of Bet Fair
And pushed some work my way

I had Jim and Honest Alf
And the use of all their boys
We had muscle and respect
I was back on my feet

And out on the street
And overseeing unpaid debt

They were glad to have me on board
And I was catching up with my past
And it was well understood
That I was very good
And I was rising high – fast

I gained control of Bet Fair
And had security on my side
The boys from Knuckle Jim
Joined me when I joined him
And then we had a firm on our side
And we expanded more
I was rising faster and higher
We had control of a few top doors
Sure
It was the start of a little empire

It's a shame Alf never got to
To see it get really big

Still there was a big turn out at his funeral

It was a very sombre day
Some had the grace to come
And others to stay away

This is only to be expected
It shows the control we now had
And that control is now respected

There was not a sound
as they lowered him
Down into the ground

Not even a stifled cough
We do look after our own
We know how to bring 'em up
And we know how to send 'em off

Far as the eye could see
White flowers – black cloth

Jim the knuckle was doing a good job
He'd brought a coach-load of boys back
down from Glasgow
Just as back up

Unlikely that anything would kick off
On a day like today
But they were there…and ready…
Just in case…

Think I saw Cherry.
Can't be sure.
I looked round to check if it was
her and she'd gone
If it was her, I'm glad
she came along

Beautiful woman
She kept me going while inside
Every night I'd think of us together
Starting a life
Maybe I'll have a look for her
Maybe I'll get myself a wife

We'll see…

Then I clap eyes on Ron
Pathetic…
decrepit
He'd gone. Gone

Couldn't climb a set of chairs without stopping
Can't even laugh without coughing

Not much of his life left

He fought for breath

Doctors gave him three weeks
That was six months ago

They don't know what's keeping him going
But that's 'cos they've no way of knowing

But I do. I know why he's hanging on

He's been hanging on for tonight

See nowadays his son is making a name for himself
Not at darts. Like his old man
No, Lee is an up and coming snooker star
Exhibitions in local pubs and halls
Hobnobbing with a page three princess
He's a big shot, flash
Likes to put himself about
Splash his cash

He's got his sights set high and he's out to win the big one at
the first attempt

I've seen a bit of him lately. Seen him play a few times and yes –
He's got a good all-round game
And he's one of the best single ball potters to have
Emerged in recent years

It's true
What they say
He's got it
Simple as
No messing

He's gonna go through
or he thinks he is anyway

Only we run things now

And he's throwing this match tonight

He's gonna lose 10-4
It'll be the shock of the draw
And the press'll put it down to fright
And in a funny way they'd be right

We've already prepped the back page of *The Sun*
'LIGHTNING LEE CHOKES WHEN IT MATTERS MOST'
The end of his career, is drawing near
When it had only just begun

He doesn't know it yet, Lee
But he soon will

We're gonna tell him. And he'll listen

And he did listen.

We explained the score
And Lightning Lee
Went down – ten frames to four

And so – on to Ron
To finish it off…
The sky bled, a cold wind blew
And I heard an old man cough

I paid him a visit – he didn't answer
So the boys kicked in the door
He panicked – 'what the fuck is it?'
'It's me, you cunt,
I'm here for you; I've come for more
Then I kicked him to the floor'

The look on his face;
The fear in his eye
He pissed and shat
and screamed and spat
As I cut him up alive

Then, I took out a rusty old dart
From the 1978 World Championships
I aimed it at his still-beating heart
And this time it did not miss

Revenge got me back my pride
It got me money, it got me power
And the revenge; it tastes so sweet

But the aftertaste is sour
And it's you that you devour

And now – look – I'm on the run
And in this way
I pay day after day
For all them things I done

Revenge is bad for your health
So if you must go looking for revenge
'Dig two graves – one for yourself.'

The End.